Girls Play to Win

BASKETBALL

by Tom Robinson

Content Consultant
Jamie Carey
Assistant Director
U.S. Women's National
Basketball Team

NORWOOD HOUSE PRESS
CHICAGO, ILLINOIS

Norwood House Press
P.O. Box 316598
Chicago, Illinois 60631

For information regarding Norwood House Press, please visit our website at:
www.norwoodhousepress.com or call 866-565-2900.

Editor: Chrös McDougall
Designer: Christa Schneider
Project Management: Red Line Editorial

Library of Congress Cataloging-in-Publication Data

Robinson, Tom.
 Girls play to win basketball / by Tom Robinson.
  p. cm. — (Girls play to win)
 Includes bibliographical references and index.
 Summary: "Covers the history, rules, fundamentals and significant personalities of the sport of women's basketball. Topics include: techniques, strategies, competitive events, and equipment. Glossary, Additional Resources and Index included"—Provided by publisher.
 ISBN-13: 978-1-59953-388-9 (library edition : alk. paper)
 ISBN-10: 1-59953-388-X (library edition : alk. paper)
 1. Women basketball players—Juvenile literature. I. Title.
 GV886.R63 2010
 796.323082—dc22
                        2010009814

Manufactured in the United States of America in North Mankato, Minnesota.
183R—042011

Girls Play to Win

BASKETBALL

Table of Contents

▲ UConn's Maya Moore cuts down the net after the 2010 national championship.

CHAPTER 1

PLAYING THE GAME

Nearly 23,000 fans filled the Alamodome in San Antonio, Texas. They had come to see one of the best college women's basketball teams ever. The University of Connecticut Huskies had won a record 77 straight games. The winning streak had spanned over three seasons. And all of those wins had been by more than 10 points. But on this day, the Huskies' streak looked to be in jeopardy.

The second-ranked Stanford University Cardinal took a 20–12 lead into halftime of the 2010 college national championship game. But when the Huskies were down, their star players stepped up. Junior forward Maya Moore ended the game with 23 points and 11 **rebounds**. Senior center Tina Charles had nine points while grabbing 11 rebounds and adding six **blocks**. The team known as UConn won 53–47. It was their seventh national championship.

College Basketball

The women who play for big schools like Connecticut and Stanford are in Division I. That is the highest level of play in women's college basketball. Many women who play at Division I schools have athletic **scholarships**. These allow athletes to play sports for colleges and universities without having to pay to go to school. The winner of the National Collegiate Athletic Association (NCAA) Division I basketball tournament is considered the best college team in the country. The tournament is a single-elimination competition that starts with the top 64 teams in the nation. With its big schools and exciting format, the tournament gets a lot of national television coverage. There are also tournaments for Division II and Division III. Division II schools can only offer partial athletic scholarships. Division III schools can offer no athletic scholarships.

"It is what great players do. And they do it at the most pressure-packed times," UConn coach Geno Auriemma said. "And that's what makes them who they are. That's what makes them great. Maya is a great scorer. And you get that reputation by scoring points under pressure. And she certainly did that."

Women's basketball is growing at a tremendous rate. Women like Moore and Charles can earn scholarships to play college basketball in front of thousands of people. When they are done, the best players have opportunities to play professionally in the Women's National Basketball Association (WNBA) and other leagues around the world. In fact, just days after winning the college national championship, the Connecticut Sun selected Charles first overall in the WNBA draft. Women can also play basketball in the Olympic Games.

The opportunities women have to play basketball today came about because of the commitment of players and leaders who helped shape the way women now play the game.

GETTING STARTED

In official basketball games, each team has five players on the court at a time. Other players are available as substitutes for when their teammates get tired. But basketball can also be played for fun at a park, in a driveway, or any other place with a basketball hoop. Basketball

▲ Connecticut's Tina Charles shoots over a Stanford defender in the 2010 national championship game.

Basketball Lingo

cut: A quick move to free a player from a defender.

drive: Dribbling the ball toward the hoop.

fast break: When one team takes possession of the ball and quickly moves it up the court before the opposing team can get its defense set up.

field goal: Another word for a basket that is not a free throw.

inside: The area closest to the basket.

jump ball: When the referee tosses the ball straight up and one player from each team jumps and tries to tip it to a teammate. It is used to start a basketball game.

outside: The area further away from the basket.

post up: Positioning one's body under the basket, or in the "low post", often with one's back to the hoop.

slam dunk: A type of shot in which the player jumps and forces the ball downward through the hoop.

hoops are set at a height of 10 feet (3.05 m) for most levels of competition. However, some youth leagues start at a lower height.

Although basketball can be played outdoors, organized games are usually played inside a gym. An official basketball court is marked with sidelines and end lines. These show the boundaries of the court. Other markings include the half-court line and center circle, the three-

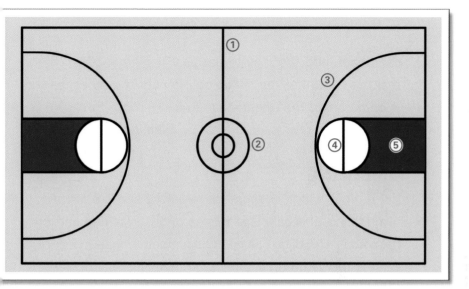

▲ This drawing of a basketball court shows the half court-line (1), center circle (2), three-point line (3), free-throw line (4), and the key (5).

point line, the free-throw line, and the free-throw lane. The free-throw lane is sometimes called the key.

Play begins with a **jump ball**. The goal of the game is to score points by shooting the ball through the hoop. Most baskets, or **field goals**, are worth two points. However, shots made from beyond the three-point line are worth three points. If a player is fouled while shooting, then she is awarded foul shots, or free throws. Each free throw made is worth one point. The player cannot be defended while shooting a free throw. When time is up, the team with the most points wins.

THE SKILLS

The basic goal of basketball might sound easy, but making a basket is harder than it looks. Before a player can shoot, she first has to get past the other team. The team in control of the ball is on offense. The other team is on defense. The offense has to try to move the ball up the court and find an open shot by **dribbling** and passing.

DRIBBLING

The ball handler cannot move unless she is bouncing, or dribbling, the ball. That makes dribbling a vital part of basketball. Dribbling can be done with either hand, but not both at the same time. How high the player bounces the ball depends on the situation. If the ball handler is running down the open court, she often bounces the ball higher because she can move faster that way. If a defender is guarding the ball handler, she will bounce the ball lower so that it is harder for the defender to steal.

A talented ball handler can keep control of the ball even against the fiercest defense. Sometimes they switch which hand bounces the ball or dribble the ball between their legs. Other times they stop and start. But dribbling almost always involves quick movements.

Bouncing the ball from one hand to the other while dribbling is called a crossover. The double crossover can be an effective way to get past a defender. In this move the ball handler quickly dribbles the ball from one hand to the other and then back again. A double crossover can throw the defender off balance, allowing the ball handler to rush past her.

This player dribbled around the screen and is headed for the hoop.

SETTING A SCREEN

A screen is a strategy that allows the player with the ball to get around the player defending her. This tactic is also sometimes called a pick. To set a screen, a teammate (the "screener") blocks the path of the defender who is guarding another player. The screener must get into position and remain still. If she is moving and bumps the defender, a foul can be called.

Often, a screen is set to help the ball handler get open. If the defensive player's path is blocked, the ball handler is free to move toward the basket. Sometimes, the defender gets around the screen and continues chasing after the ball handler. In that case, the screener **pivots** or "rolls" past the defensive player and makes herself open for a pass.

Screens can also be set for players who don't have the ball. This is called an off-ball screen. The off-ball screen allows the teammate to get around her defender and get open for a pass.

The Positions

Most basketball teams have a point guard, two wings/guards, and two post players. However, some teams use different combinations depending on the makeup of their team.

The point guard is the playmaker on a basketball team. She is usually in charge of bringing the ball up the court and finding an open teammate to pass to. A good point guard has very good ball-handling skills and is also skilled at passing. The other guards/wings often play further away from the basket, too. Offensively, they need to be able to shoot from greater distances or use dribbling to **drive** quickly toward the basket.

The posts are often taller than the guards and play nearer to the basket. Sometimes they are called forwards and centers. A post player's role is to grab rebounds, block **inside shots**, and score from under the basket.

Advanced players use all sorts of ball handling tricks to fool defenders. Some players can even move the ball from one side of their body to the other by wrapping it around their own back. Others blow by defenders by spinning while dribbling the ball.

PASSING

Teamwork is key in basketball. The best way to get teammates involved on offense is by passing the ball. Passing moves the ball to an open player. Teams can also move the ball around the defense quickly with a series of passes, often opening up new spaces to create open shots in the process.

There are different kinds of passes. The most common is the chest pass. This is when a player pushes the ball from her chest to an open teammate. The bounce pass can sometimes be a more effective way to move the ball through a tight space. A bounce pass is like a chest pass, only the ball bounces off the floor about two-thirds of the way between players. This makes it harder to defend against. Overhead passes can move the ball longer distances or start a fast break.

Advanced players can get creative with their passing. Sometimes a player can trick a defender by completing a no-look pass, which is exactly what it sounds like. Sometimes players can even pass the ball around their own back.

SHOOTING

Once a player is open, she can shoot the ball. The type of shot she takes is often based on where she is on the court. The easiest shot to make is the layup. These are close-range shots that are usually made on the run. A player who gets close enough to the hoop will jump and lightly toss the ball toward the center of the backboard. The ball then bounces off the backboard and into the hoop.

▲ *Kelly Mazzante puts up a jump shot in a 2009 WNBA game.*

Although layups are more likely to go in than other shots, they require the player to get past the defense first.

If a player is not close to the basket, she can take either a set shot or a jump shot. In a set shot, the player steadies the ball with one hand and then flicks the wrist on her dominant hand to release the ball. **Three-point shots** are often set shots because they give the shooter more strength. Most players use set shots to shoot free throws, too. A jump shot is similar to a set shot. The main difference is that the shooter releases the ball at the top of a jump.

Shots are always more likely to go in if the shooter is open. However, advanced players can adjust their shots if they are heavily defended. One way is with a fade-away jump shot. By jumping and leaning backward, a player can free up some space from the defender while she shoots.

DEFENSE

Once the offense loses possession of the ball, the offensive players immediately have to switch to defense. There are two main types of defense in basketball: zone and man-to-man. In a zone defense, each player defends an area, or zone. A zone defense can be helpful when the other team has a star player who is hard for one defender to guard. The 2–3 zone defense is the most common. That

Rebounding

When shots are missed, both teams try to retrieve the ball. This is known as rebounding. If the offensive team gets the ball back, they are allowed to shoot again. If the defensive team secures the rebound, they head in the other direction to try to score at the other basket.

The best way to get in position to grab a rebound is by **boxing out**. To do this, once a shot is in the air, the player will face the basket. She then positions herself in between the basket and an opposing player. By setting her body like that, the player "boxes out" the opposing player. That keeps the opposing player from getting into a good position to make the rebound.

is when two players defend the area around the foul line while three players defend the area under the basket.

Man-to-man defense is a more aggressive defense. In this system, each player is responsible for guarding one player on the other team. Sometimes coaches like their players to stay on one opponent no matter what. Others expect players to switch who they are guarding when an offensive player **cuts** or uses a screen.

No matter what type of defense a team uses, the goal is ultimately to stop the offense from scoring a basket. The best way to do that is to keep pressure on the offensive players at all times. Good defenders can steal the ball from an opposing dribbler or intercept an opponent's pass. If the opponent begins to take a shot, the defender raises her arms to try to block the shot or the shooter's view of the basket. Even if she does not block it, putting pressure on the shooter makes her more likely to miss.

Although some physical contact happens during a basketball game, players are not allowed to hold, grab, or push each other. Doing any of those results in a foul. Depending on the league, a player has to leave the game if she commits five or six fouls.

Once the defending team gets the ball back, that team goes back on offense and tries to score again. But the game of basketball moves quickly, so there is no standing around.

▲ This player prepares to guard the opponent's point guard.

▲ *This girls' basketball team from Washington D.C. played in 1899.*

CHAPTER 2

THE EARLY DAYS

Dr. James Naismith is credited with inventing basketball. In December 1891, Naismith was looking for a way to entertain rowdy young men at the Young Men's Christian Association (YMCA) training school in Springfield, Massachusetts. He came up with a new game that he called "basket ball." It was somewhat different from basketball as it is played today. The hoops were peach baskets hung on either side of the gym. Players did not dribble, but passed the ball down the court toward the goal. In the first basketball games, there were nine players on each side. Today the standard number of players is five. Naismith's game soon caught on in other parts of the country. In 1892, it caught the attention of Senda Berenson. She was a gymnastics instructor and physical education teacher at Smith College, an all-women's school in Northampton, Massachusetts.

Berenson read an article Naismith wrote about the game. She wondered whether it would be an appropriate activity for the women in her physical education classes. It was not such a simple question at the time. Berenson taught during an era when women were not allowed to vote in elections. Many people thought that women were inferior to men. They believed that women should not take part in any physically demanding activity because they could not handle it. So, before Berenson introduced the game in her classes, she changed the rules. Berenson's version better fit the standards of a game women would be allowed to play at the time.

WOMEN'S BASKETBALL BEGINS

Berenson decided that each team should have six players. She divided the court into three areas—the offense, defense, and the middle—and required each player to stay in her area. That meant the players did not need to run so frequently up and down the court. To eliminate overly aggressive actions, snatching the ball from

Basquette

In 1893, physical education teacher Clara Gregory Baer introduced basketball to women at Sophie Newcomb College in New Orleans, Louisiana. She called the game "basquette" and used slightly different rules from the ones Berenson was teaching in Massachusetts. For example, women playing basquette could not dribble or guard each other. The court was also divided based on the number of players rather than Berenson's standard three sections. In 1895, Baer published the first set of women's basketball rules.

another player was forbidden. Berenson urged teamwork and tried to reduce the strain on the women's bodies. Women were also allowed to dribble. However, the rules required a player to give up the ball after dribbling three times or holding the ball for three seconds.

Women's basketball was first played during Berenson's classes. But before long there were more formal games being arranged. At Smith College, a team of sophomores (second-year students) played a team of freshmen (first-year students) in the first public **intramural** game in March 1893. With baskets counting as one point each, the freshmen beat the sophomores 5–4. Men were not invited, however. It was not socially acceptable for them to watch women play sports.

▲ *Women at Smith College playing basketball around the turn of the 20th century*

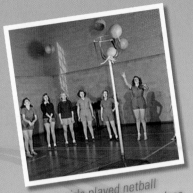
These girls played netball during physical education class.

NETBALL

Netball is a game similar to the style of women's basketball originally played in the United States. Players are limited to certain parts of the court. They may dribble once and must pass within three seconds. The ball is shot at a hoop at the top of a pole rather than attached to a backboard. Otherwise, the game is played much like modern basketball. Girls' netball is still popular in the British Commonwealth, particularly in Australia, New Zealand, Jamaica, and the United Kingdom.

SPREADING THE GAME

Although the game started in the northeast, it soon spread to other parts of the country as well. Teams from the University of California and Anna Head School, both located in Berkeley, California, played against each other in November 1892. It was less than a year after the game had been invented.

By 1895, women were playing basketball at colleges in Massachusetts, New York, Pennsylvania, and even Louisiana. As the game spread, new groups of players debated the rules. One of the issues they discussed was how many players should be on each team. They also discussed whether they should play Berenson's version or the men's version. They even discussed what types of shots and throws were proper for ladies. At the time, women were not allowed to throw two-handed chest passes or shots. Some people thought that would restrict their breathing.

High school girls in Illinois got a jump start on boys in basketball. Chicago's Austin High School started a girls' team in the fall of 1895 that played against college teams. Austin then faced Oak Park High on December 18, 1896. The game was played primarily following the men's rules for basketball. That was the first girls' basketball game between two high schools in the country. It was also the first high school basketball game—boys' or girls'—in Illinois.

First Intercollegiate Game

Stanford University and the University of California met for the first **intercollegiate** women's basketball game on April 4, 1896. Women were stationed at the windows and doors to make sure men would not disrupt their game. The teams played with nine players on a side—three in each zone—and the rules held that no player could run more than five feet (1.524 m) at a time. With each basket counting as one point, Stanford won 2–1.

Game Ball

Girls' and women's basketball is played with a ball that is between 28.5 and 29 inches (72.39–73.66 cm) around. That size is one inch less than the ball used for boys' and men's basketball. Women on average have smaller hands than men, and the slight difference in size helps female players handle the ball better.

Women had other hurdles to overcome in playing basketball. They had originally played in long dresses. But that made athletic movement difficult. Some movements were discouraged, such as getting down on the floor to grab a loose ball.

They also had to deal with opposition from people who did not support women's sports. In 1908, the **Amateur** Athletic Union (AAU) adopted the position that women should not play basketball in public. The AAU then declared its opposition to allowing women to play in the Olympics. Despite these obstacles, the women continued to push forward and advance the game.

▲ *The pioneers of women's basketball wore much different uniforms than today's players.*

▲ This girls' basketball team, with their coach, played around 1910.

CHAPTER 3

GOING NATIONAL

Women's basketball continued to grow after the first high school game in 1896. In 1919, the AAU gave up its resistance to public play by women. The organization conducted a basketball tournament for its Central Region in Chicago. The regional championship was played with teams of five, according to men's rules.

In 1926, the Pasadena Athletic and Country Club team emerged from a field of six entries to win the first AAU Women's National Championship. Pasadena defeated Anaheim 11–10 in the championship game.

The AAU sponsored the first national women's basketball championship in 1926. It was held in Pasadena, California, with only six teams participating. The second tournament was held two years later, in 1928. This time it was in Wichita, Kansas. There were 25 teams. The AAU tournament would remain in Wichita for the next 11 years.

The game was reaching the national level for the first time. Settling on rules became important. Most high school and college teams around the country were following women's rules, as outlined by Clara Baer. That meant they were playing the game in two or three zones and with six or nine players. But the AAU teams were following men's rules. They had five players to a team. It was decided in 1928 that the AAU would follow women's rules. Their games now had six players on a side in three zones. Following the end of World War II in 1945, these rules were altered. That eventually created the women's game we know today.

▲ *Women playing basketball in 1926*

Teams from Dallas, Texas, dominated the first four tournaments in Wichita. In 1931, legendary athlete Mildred "Babe" Didrikson led the Dallas Golden Cyclones to the AAU National Championship. She also became the sport's first star along the way. Didrikson scored 106 points in five games and helped her team beat the Wichita Thurstons 28–26 in the final.

TRAVELING SHOW

Women's basketball was growing in popularity. But without a professional league or national college championship, there were few opportunities to continue playing at a high level. Some **elite** women found other ways to continue playing.

Babe Didrikson-Zaharias was a star athlete in many sports.

BABE DIDRIKSON-ZAHARIAS

Mildred "Babe" Didrikson was born in Texas in 1911. Didrikson went against expectations for women of her time when she set out to be the greatest athlete who ever lived. She excelled in many sports, including basketball, track and field, golf, baseball, tennis, swimming, volleyball, and figure skating. Before basketball was part of the Olympics, Didrikson qualified for the 1932 Olympic Games in five track and field events. However, women were only able to compete in three events at the time. Didrikson still took home one silver and two gold medals. Didrikson was also a founding member of the Ladies Professional Golf Association (LPGA), formed in 1950. In 1954, Didrikson won her third U.S. Women's Open golf title by 12 strokes.

The Associated Press *named her Female Athlete of the Year six times, and in 1950, they honored her as the Greatest Female Athlete of the first half of the 20th century. In 1938, Didrikson married professional wrestler George Zaharias and became known as Babe Didrikson-Zaharias. She died of cancer in 1956 at the age of 45.*

Nera White

Tennessean Nera White was responsible for leading the first national **dynasty** in women's basketball. White began playing on an amateur team sponsored by the Nashville Business College in 1954. Her team won ten AAU National Championship titles in 11 years, including eight straight titles from 1962 to 1969. She also helped Team USA win the 1957 World Championship in Brazil.

White was 6 feet 1 inch (1.85 m) tall. Her height made her an unstoppable force under the basket. She also had a great ability to find and pass to teammates. In 1992, White became the first woman inducted into the National Basketball Hall of Fame.

The most famous teams of the 1930s and 1940s were traveling teams that played **exhibitions**. Didrikson continued playing on the AAU championship team, the Golden Cyclones. A promoter offered Didrikson a place as the only female member of a team he named the Babe Didrikson All-Americans. They traveled around the country playing exhibitions in front of large crowds. Didrikson was the star attraction.

One of the first women's professional basketball teams was the All-American Red Heads. They were formed in Cassville, Missouri, in 1936. To fit their name, all the women had red hair. Those who were not naturally redheads dyed their locks. The All-American Red Heads played many of their games against men. The team moved its base to Carraway, Arkansas, in 1955. There, they were led by new owner and coach Orwell "Red" Moore. His wife, Lorene "Butch" Moore, scored 35,246 career points for the team and played in more than 2,000 games. Except during World War II (1941–1945), the Red Heads played from 1936 through 1986.

The Texas Cowgirls were another women's exhibition team. They played from 1949 to 1977. Like the Red Heads, they also played against men's teams and followed men's rules. The Cowgirls often opened for National Basketball Association (NBA) teams and the Harlem Globetrotters.

GOING GLOBAL

Basketball was introduced to the world as a demonstration event at the 1904 Olympic Games. Men's basketball officially became an Olympic sport at the 1936 Olympics in Berlin, Germany. Although most basketball is played during the winter months, the sport is played in the summer Olympics. Women's basketball would not debut in the Olympics for another 40 years. But women did have another international competition.

FIBA, the International Basketball Federation, created the World Championship for Women in 1953. The United States won the first two championships—in 1953 and in 1957. The former Soviet Union won the next five titles in 1959, 1964, 1967, 1971, and 1975. But as of 2009, the

United States has the most titles of any nation: seven. The event is now held every four years instead of every three.

COLLEGE BASKETBALL

The growth of international women's basketball was followed by growth in the United States. The Commission on Intercollegiate Athletics for Women (CIAW) held the first national college women's basketball tournament in 1969. The first two tournaments were played in the six-player format before switching to the five-player game in 1971. The tournaments continued until 1982 under the Association for Intercollegiate Athletics for Women (AIAW). They were then folded into the NCAA.

More Rule Changes

Most women's basketball games in the United States switched from a three-section court to a two-section court in 1938. Six-player teams became the norm. In 1971, the majority of the nation—including the new National College Championship—adopted the five-player team playing the full-court game that is used by all players today. That same year, a 30-second shot clock was introduced. The shot clock sped up the action and prevented teams from delaying the game. The last major change to basketball was the addition of the three-point line. It became more widespread during the 1980s after the NBA began using it.

▲ Sue Bird starred for Team USA during the 2000s.

▲ *Title IX gave a boost to college women's basketball teams.*

CHAPTER 4

MARCHING
TO THE FRONT

President Richard Nixon signed Title IX of the Education Amendment of 1972 into law on June 23, 1972. Title IX was originally drafted to give equal educational opportunities to both men and women. Today, the amendment is known for its effect on sports. Title IX said that schools and colleges that receive government funds have to work to provide equal sporting opportunities for men and women. The opportunities for girls to play sports—

and the number of girls playing them—greatly increased after Title IX was passed.

Individual schools began to create many more teams for girls. As public schools added girls' and women's sports, private institutions have made changes to keep up. The public schools needed to make sure those teams had facilities, equipment, and financial commitment similar to those of boys' teams. State high school and national college organizations scrambled to put together women's

Mighty Macs

Immaculata College was the first national power in the championship era of women's college basketball. Immaculata is a small private school located just west of Philadelphia, Pennsylvania. In 1972, Immaculata was able to overcome local rival West Chester State 52–48 in the championship game. The title was the first of three straight for Immaculata. The "Mighty Macs" finished second in 1975 and 1976 and fourth in 1977. Immaculata also had the distinction of winning the first nationally televised women's basketball game and the first game at the famous Madison Square Garden in New York City. Immaculata defeated the University of Maryland 80–48 on television in January 1975. A month later, the team beat Queens College 65–61 at Madison Square Garden. A crowd of 11,969 fans came out to the game. Although the school used to compete at the top level, it became Immaculata University in 2002 and now competes at the NCAA Division III level.

championship tournaments to match those already in place for male athletes. The number of college athletic scholarships for women skyrocketed, too. Before Title IX, they were almost nonexistent for women. Women's basketball was one of many sports that benefited greatly from Title IX.

GROWTH OF THE COLLEGE GAME

During the early stages of Title IX, the AIAW replaced the CIAW. The AIAW held its first National Championship tournament in basketball in 1972. One year later, it began allowing athletic scholarships. However, not all schools were able to offer scholarships.

The AIAW responded by making multiple tournaments. They were divided according to if and how schools offered scholarships. The AIAW added a second division in 1975 and a third division in 1978. The biggest schools that also offered scholarships were in the top division.

Two Champions

The NCAA held its first Division I women's basketball national championship in 1982. That was at the same time the AIAW conducted its last tournament. Louisiana Tech won the tournament run by the NCAA. Rutgers was the AIAW's last national champion.

▲ *Louisiana Tech coach Sonja Hogg was carried off the court after her team won the AIAW championship in 1981, one year before winning the first NCAA tournament.*

The organization ran its last championship tournament in 1982. At that point, the NCAA took over the administration of women's collegiate sports. The schools found it was more convenient to work with the NCAA because it could serve as the governing body for both men's and women's athletics. The NCAA has since overseen both men's and women's athletic competition for the vast majority of four-year colleges in the United States. When the AIAW lost a court battle with the NCAA in 1982, it no longer had a reason to operate, and disbanded.

▲ *Old Dominion's Nancy Lieberman (right) steals the ball from a Louisiana Tech player in 1979.*

YOUNG STARS

The expansion on the high school level also helped spark other growth in women's basketball. The International Olympic Committee added women's basketball to the 1976 Olympic Games in Montreal, Canada. There, 18-year-old American Nancy Lieberman helped Team USA win a silver medal. That jump-started a Hall of Fame career for Lieberman.

Lieberman grew up in Brooklyn, New York. She developed into a tough and aggressive player. Although she could score, Lieberman was best known for the passing and dribbling skills she displayed as point guard. Following the 1976 Olympics, Lieberman went on to star at Old Dominion University in Virginia. She led Old Dominion to two national titles while picking up two national player of the year awards along the way.

After college, Lieberman starred in various women's professional basketball leagues. She also spent some time in the minor league men's United States Basketball League. Lieberman was the first woman to play in an all-men's league when she played for the Springfield Fame in 1986. She also played for the Long Island Knights men's team in 1987. Then, in 1988, Lieberman joined the Washington Generals and toured the world playing against the Harlem Globetrotters, both of which are men's teams that perform exhibitions around the world.

Olympic Success

Team USA won its first Olympic title in 1984. That began a winning streak of six gold medals in seven Olympics. They only missed out on gold at the 1992 Olympics in Barcelona, Spain. But Team USA still finished with a bronze medal that year.

First Dunk

Georgeann Wells stood 6 feet 7 inches (2.00 m) tall as a center at West Virginia University. She is credited with the first **slam dunk** in women's college basketball history. She completed the feat during a win over in-state rival College of Charleston on December 21, 1984.

Lieberman was enshrined in the Naismith Memorial Basketball Hall of Fame in 1996. But she did not stop there. In 1997, she played in the WNBA's first season as a member of the Phoenix Mercury. After serving as a coach and general manager, she made one more brief return to playing with the Detroit Shock in 2008. Lieberman was one of the first stars of women's basketball and is considered a great pioneer for the game.

Ann Meyers was another standout player during the 1970s. Meyers won a silver medal with Team USA at the 1976 Olympics. She also earned All-America honors four times at the University of California, Los Angeles. After that she earned a tryout with the NBA's Indiana Pacers in 1979. However, she was unable to secure a roster spot on the men's professional team.

Carol Blazejowski led the nation in scoring while playing at Montclair State University in New Jersey. Known as "The Blaze," she averaged 31.7 points per game in her

▲ *Ann Meyers goes for a layup while practicing with the Indiana Pacers in 1979.*

career—a women's college record. Blazejowski averaged 33.5 points in the 1976–77 season and 38.6 points in the 1977–78 season to win scoring titles. Her 1977–78 scoring average still stands as a college women's record, as well. She had 3,199 career points.

TURNING PRO

Women's college basketball was developing a lot of talented players through the 1970s. Organizers soon decided to try building the game on the professional level, too. The process was difficult at first. The Women's Professional Basketball League (WBL) was the first widely recognized league of its kind. It began in 1978, but the organization disbanded at the end of the 1980–1981 season. The teams did not earn enough money to pay the players.

The Women's Basketball Association (WBA) started in the summer of 1993. The league held its season during the summer to avoid competing with the more established NBA and college basketball for fans. The WBA experienced the same problems as the WBL, though, and lasted for only three seasons.

In 1996, two new leagues emerged. The WNBA announced that it would begin play in June 1997. The WNBA was the first league to have the NBA's support. WNBA teams would play in existing NBA arenas and have other benefits from the established men's league.

Cheryl Miller helped Team USA beat South Korea in the 1984 Olympic gold-medal game.

STARS OF THE 1980s

The 1980s saw very talented female players take to the court. Cheryl Miller was a three-time national Player of the Year at the University of Southern California (USC). She helped USC win the 1983 and 1984 NCAA Tournaments. Then she led Team USA to an Olympic gold medal in 1984. Miller scored 3,018 points and grabbed 1,534 rebounds in her four years at USC. She often drew additional attention because of her flashy, sometimes showboating, style of play.

Standing 6 feet 8 inches (2.03 m) tall, Anne Donovan arrived at Old Dominion in 1979. She played center while Nancy Lieberman was still there. Donovan left as a national champion and the school's all-time leader in points, rebounds, and blocked shots. Donovan missed her first opportunity to win an Olympic medal when the United States boycotted the 1980 Olympic Games in Moscow, Soviet Union. But she went on to win gold medals at the 1984 and 1988 Olympic Games.

Meanwhile, the American Basketball League (ABL) started late in 1996. The ABL attempted to build off the popularity of Team USA's victory in the 1996 Olympic Games in Atlanta, Georgia. Unlike the WNBA, the ABL used the traditional winter basketball season. The ABL made it through two seasons. However, the league folded in December 1998 during the early stages of its third season.

New sports leagues often struggle to earn more money than they spend early on. With help from the NBA's financial resources, the WNBA was able to overcome that. The WNBA signed its first player on October 23, 1996. She was a good one. In 1993, Sheryl Swoopes had scored a record 47 points during an NCAA championship game, leading her team, Texas Tech University, to an 84–82 victory over Ohio State. With its first star in place, the WNBA moved forward as an established women's league.

▲ *Sheryl Swoopes looks for an open teammate in a 1999 WNBA game.*

▲ (From left to right) Tina Thompson, Sheryl Swoopes, and Cynthia Cooper—three of the Houston Comets who won the first four WNBA titles

CHAPTER 5

ON TOP OF THE GAME

Cynthia Cooper won two NCAA national championships while at the University of Southern California. She also won the 1988 Olympic gold medal with Team USA. When she joined the Houston Comets for the WNBA's first season, the success only continued.

Cooper was the league's Most Valuable Player (MVP) during its first two seasons, in 1997 and 1998. She also guided the Comets to playoff success. Cooper, along with fellow stars Sheryl Swoopes and Tina Thompson, guided the Comets to victory in the first four WNBA Finals. Cooper was named MVP of the WNBA Finals all four times. "Cynthia was the Michael Jordan of the WNBA," said former Houston Comets owner Leslie Alexander. "We won four championships and Cynthia was the main reason."

FINDING STABILITY

By 2000, women's basketball was a firmly established sport. The WNBA was more stable than any of the past professional women's basketball leagues. College women's basketball also had well-established tournaments on three levels. The NCAA had previously been accused of neglecting women's sports. Now, the organization was nurturing the women's basketball tournament by promoting it more and expanding it so that there were as many teams as were in the men's tournament.

Check the Shoes

After leading her team to the 1993 national title, Sheryl Swoopes became the first woman to have a basketball shoe named after her. Nike created "Air Swoopes" in 1994. She led the United States to three Olympic gold medals. And from 1997 to 2000, Swoopes helped the Houston Comets win four straight WNBA titles.

Basketball was one of the few options for girls in high school sports prior to Title IX. By the turn of the 21st century, Title IX had been in effect for more than 25 years. The barriers that once made it hard for girls to find a team to play for had long been removed. State high school associations had begun naming multiple state champions according to school size. Girls were also playing basketball using the same rules as boys without objection.

Since Title IX, girls were being introduced to basketball at increasingly younger ages. This improved their

WNBA's Best Shot

The Houston Comets and New York Liberty met in the 1999 WNBA Finals, a best-of-three championship series. Houston had won the first game and was close to winning the second when New York's Teresa Weatherspoon made an amazing shot.

Houston was leading 67–65 with only 2.4 seconds left in the game. Weatherspoon took an in-bound pass from Kym Hampton. She quickly dribbled to the right sideline near midcourt and let the ball fly. Although she was half a court away—approximately 50 feet (15.24 m) from the basket—Weatherspoon's last-second shot miraculously went in, giving New York a 68–67 win. The team had another chance to win the series, but Houston clinched the title. Nevertheless, when the WNBA celebrated its first decade in 2006, fans voted Weatherspoon's shot as the greatest in league history.

chances of learning organized basketball before reaching high school. The overall number of girls playing the sport was increasing, too. As a result, the quality of play was improving across the country.

COLLEGE POWERS

Before the WNBA emerged as a stable professional women's basketball league, college basketball was the most consistent showcase of the sport. Even with the WNBA, the college game still sometimes gets more attention than the professional game. Part of that is because of the NCAA Tournament. Today, the top 64 teams compete in a single-elimination tournament for the national title. That means that a team is eliminated after it loses one game. Since the women's and men's tournaments both take place mostly during March, they are nicknamed March Madness.

Certain schools have attracted a lot of attention over the years. The University of Tennessee has long been a powerhouse in women's college basketball. And legendary coach Pat Summitt led the way. She took over as coach for the 1974–75 season. After that, the Tennessee Lady Volunteers went on to win eight national championships. On February 5, 2009, she became the first NCAA coach to win 1,000 games. No other coach in college basketball—men's or women's—has won as many games as Summitt.

▲ *University of Tennessee players dump confetti on coach Pat Summitt after her 1,000th career victory.*

The University of Connecticut has challenged Tennessee for NCAA dominance. From 2000 to 2010, Connecticut won six national titles to Tennessee's two. At that time, Connecticut had seven national championships while Tennessee had eight. A rivalry developed between the two universities that became one of the most heated in women's team sports.

A Women's First

In 1990, Tennessee coach Pat Summitt became the first female winner of the John Bunn Lifetime Achievement Award from the Basketball Hall of Fame. Bunn was the first chairman of the Basketball Hall of Fame. The award is considered one of the most prestigious honors given out by the Hall of Fame.

Connecticut set a record by winning 70 straight games from 2001 to 2003. The team broke that record during the 2009–10 season. After winning the 2010 national title, the team had 78 straight wins. The Connecticut Huskies captured the attention of an entire state—and basketball fans nationwide—during that decade. Players such as Sue Bird, Swin Cash, Tina Charles, Rebecca Lobo, Maya Moore, and Diana Taurasi were among those who starred for the school nicknamed UConn.

Tennessee and Connecticut have led the sport in more than just wins. They also draw big crowds. During the 2008–09 season, those teams had the highest attendance at home games. An average Tennessee home game drew a crowd of 13,999. Connecticut averaged 10,514. Iowa State, the University of Oklahoma, Purdue University, Texas Tech University, and the University of Maryland were the next largest. They all averaged more than 8,000 fans per home game.

WNBA STARS

After Cooper, Swoopes, and Thompson led the Houston Comets to four straight titles, new teams and new stars have taken over. Standing at a height of 6 feet 5 inches (1.96 m), Lisa Leslie led the Los Angeles Sparks to back-to-back titles in 2001 and 2002. She was the first WNBA player to capture all three MVP awards—regular season, all-star game, and playoff finals—in the same season. The star center scored more points than any player in league history before retiring in 2009.

Another star joined Leslie on the Sparks in 2008. The team drafted Candace Parker first overall in the WNBA Draft. Parker had led the University of Tennessee to back-to-back national titles in 2007 and 2008. She is credited with dunking seven times, the most in college women's basketball history. Upon joining the Sparks, Parker became the first WNBA player to be named MVP and Rookie of the Year in the same season.

Diana Taurasi was one of the most dominant college basketball players ever. She helped Connecticut to three straight NCAA titles from 2002–04. The Phoenix Mercury selected Taurasi first overall in the 2004 WNBA Draft. She immediately showed her talent in the pros, being named **First Team All-WNBA** as a rookie. The guard/forward also won gold medals in the 2004 and 2008 Olympics. She was named the MVP of the 2009 WNBA finals when she led the Mercury to the championship.

▲ *Lisa Leslie was a three-time WNBA MVP and four-time Olympic gold medalist for Team USA.*

▲ *Angel McCoughtry dribbles the ball around a defender in a 2009 WNBA game. She was the 2009 WNBA Rookie of the Year.*

Angel McCoughtry led the University of Louisville, from Kentucky, to the championship game of the NCAA Tournament in 2009. It was the school's first appearance in the championship game. They lost the championship to Connecticut. But that summer, she was picked first in the WNBA draft. She then earned Rookie of the Year honors playing for the Atlanta Dream.

Chamique Holdsclaw was a six-time WNBA All-Star.

WINNING BIG

Chamique Holdsclaw played on championship teams for seven straight years. She won four New York State titles at Christ the King High School in Queens, New York. She then won NCAA titles in her first three years playing for Pat Summitt at the University of Tennessee. Holdsclaw scored 3,025 career points and was named National Player of the Year twice at Tennessee.

In 1999, Holdsclaw became the first women's basketball player to win the Sullivan Award as the nation's top amateur athlete. The Washington Mystics selected her first in the 1999 WNBA Draft. Holdsclaw went on to a successful WNBA career with the Mystics, Los Angeles Sparks, and Atlanta Dream. She also won the Olympic gold medal in 2000.

Finding Its Place

The WNBA has been better accepted in some cities than others. Although the Houston Comets were a successful team, they did not make enough money. The league began managing the Comets franchise in 2008. But when it could not find new ownership, the WNBA shut down its original powerhouse following the 2008 season.

The WNBA started with eight teams and grew to as many as 16. But the league entered the 2010 season with 12 teams. Six teams have shut down through the years. The Orlando Miracle made a successful move to become the Connecticut Sun in 2003. That same year, the Utah Starzz became the San Antonio Silver Stars. The Detroit Shock relocated to Oklahoma and became the Tulsa Shock after the 2009 season. Some of the teams are no longer affiliated with an NBA franchise. They now have independent ownership.

Over the past several years, girls and women have improved the quality of play on every level, from high school, to college, to the pros, to the Olympics. As they have improved, so has the fan interest. Thanks to some of the top college programs, the top women's players are used to playing in front of large crowds. With a strong foundation already in place, there is nowhere to go but up for aspiring women's basketball players.

▲ Candace Parker takes the ball up court for the Los Angeles Sparks in the 2009 WNBA playoffs.

GLOSSARY

amateur: Refers to athletes who have never competed for money.

blocks: When a defender stops an opposing shot before it reaches the basket.

boxing out: A position that blocks the opposing player from grabbing a rebound.

cuts: Quick movements to free a player from a defender.

dribbling: Bouncing the ball repeatedly with one hand to move from one spot to another.

drive: To dribble toward the basket.

dynasty: A group of people, or team, that is successful over a long period of time.

elite: The best of the best.

exhibitions: Non-competitive games that are often played for the audience's enjoyment.

field goals: Baskets other than foul shots; they are worth two points unless taken from beyond the three-point line.

First Team All-WNBA: An award given to the top players in the Women's National Basketball Association.

inside shots: Shots taken from close to the basket.

intercollegiate: Intercollegiate games are competitions between teams from different colleges.

intramural: Intramural games are competitions between teams from the same school.

jump ball: The start of a game when the referee throws the ball up between a player from each team and then they try to tip it to a teammate.

pivots: Rotations while keeping one foot planted on the ground to avoid traveling.

rebounds: Retrieved missed shots.

scholarships: Money given to students to help them pay for classes or other college expenses as a reward for skills in specific areas, such as athletics.

slam dunk: A type of shot in which the player jumps and forces the ball downward through the hoop.

three-point shots: Baskets made on a shot from beyond the arc used to determine one additional point.

FOR MORE INFORMATION

BOOKS

Frost, Shelley. *Throw Like a Girl: Discovering the Body, Mind, and Spirit of the Athlete in You.* Hillsboro, OR: Beyond Words, 2000.
This book encourages girls to become better athletes.

Roberts, Robin. *Basketball Year: What It's Like to Be a Woman Pro.* Brookfield, CT: Millbrook, 2000.
This book explains what life is like for women who play in the WNBA.

Schaller, Bob, and Dave Harnish. *The Everything Kids' Basketball Book.* Avon, MA: Adams Media, 2009.
This guidebook includes all types of information about basketball.

Weatherspoon, Teresa. *Teresa Weatherspoon's Basketball for Girls.* New York: John Wiley, 1999.
WNBA player Weatherspoon teaches girls about basketball while providing examples from her own life and career.

WEB SITES

History of Women's Basketball
www.wnba.com/about_us/jenkins_feature.html
This Web page has an in-depth report and timeline chronicling the history of women's basketball.

Naismith Memorial Basketball Hall of Fame
www.hoophall.com
This Web site contains information about the greatest basketball players ever to play the game.

NCAA
www.ncaa.com
The official Web site of the National Collegiate Athletic Association has information on college sports and their national championships.

WNBA
www.wnba.com
The official Web site of the Women's National Basketball Association has team rosters, schedules, standings, statistics, and more.

Women's Basketball Museum
www.womensbasketballmuseum.com
This Web site has photos and information about the early years of women's basketball.

INDEX

PLACES TO VISIT

Naismith Memorial Basketball Hall of Fame

1000 W. Columbus Avenue, Springfield, MA 01105
(413) 781-6500
www.hoophall.com
The museum features interactive exhibits that document the history of basketball, as well as skill challenges, live clinics, and more.

U.S. Olympic Training Center

One Olympic Plaza, Colorado Springs, CO 80909
www.teamusa.org
(888) 659-8687 or (719) 866-4618
The Olympic Training Center offers free public tours that include a video and a walking tour of the complex, showcasing the training facilities for the U.S. Olympic and Paralympic hopefuls who train there.

ABOUT THE AUTHOR

Tom Robinson is a freelance writer and editor of educational material. He has written more than 20 nonfiction books, most of which were created for young readers. During his long career as a sports writer, Robinson has covered women's basketball on the high school and college level.

ABOUT THE CONTENT CONSULTANT

Jamie Carey is the assistant director of the U.S. women's national basketball team. She played basketball for Stanford University and the University of Texas before playing four seasons with the Connecticut Sun in the WNBA. Carey also played for Team USA in 1998, 2003, and 2007.